Finding Out About
ROCKETS AND SPACEFLIGHT

Contents

Written by:

Lynn Myring

Designed by:

Roger Priddy
Iain Ashman
Kim Blundell

Illustrated by:

Martin Newton
Louise Nevett
Philip Schramm

Consultant editors:

Carole Turpie
Ian Ridpath

About spaceflight

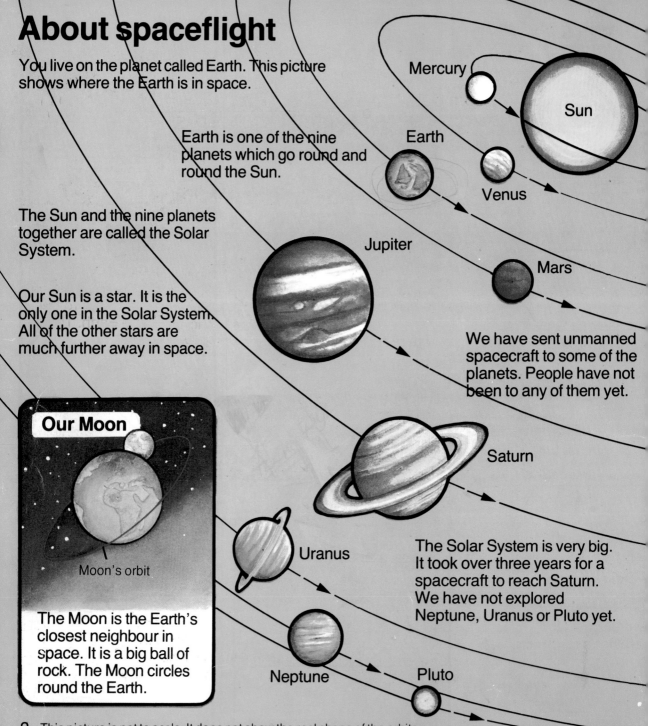

You live on the planet called Earth. This picture shows where the Earth is in space.

Earth is one of the nine planets which go round and round the Sun.

The Sun and the nine planets together are called the Solar System.

Our Sun is a star. It is the only one in the Solar System. All of the other stars are much further away in space.

We have sent unmanned spacecraft to some of the planets. People have not been to any of them yet.

The Solar System is very big. It took over three years for a spacecraft to reach Saturn. We have not explored Neptune, Uranus or Pluto yet.

Mercury

Sun

Earth

Venus

Jupiter

Mars

Saturn

Uranus

Neptune

Pluto

Our Moon

Moon's orbit

The Moon is the Earth's closest neighbour in space. It is a big ball of rock. The Moon circles round the Earth.

2 This picture is not to scale. It does not show the real shape of the orbits.

Leaving the Earth

Gravity pulls like a big magnet.

Orbit

Getting off the Earth is the hardest part of a space journey. A strong force called gravity tries to pull the spacecraft back down.

Gravity is what makes things fall to the ground. It is gravity which keeps things on the Earth and stops them flying out to space.

Gravity even affects spacecraft close to the Earth. It makes them circle round and round the Earth. This is called orbiting.

Planning space journeys

Sending a spacecraft to the Moon or a planet is hard because the Earth, Moon and planets are moving all the time. A space journey has to be very carefully planned. It is controlled by lots of people and computers.

A space journey takes so long that a planet will have moved before the spacecraft gets to it. The spacecraft has to be aimed at the place where the planet will be at the end of its journey.

3

Rockets

A rocket is a very strong kind of engine. It is the only kind powerful enough to fight gravity and launch a spacecraft into space.

The picture below shows a spacecraft and its big launching rockets.

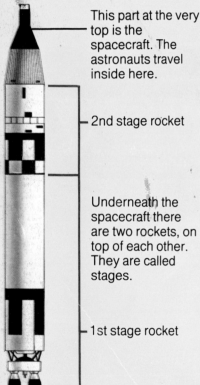

This part at the very top is the spacecraft. The astronauts travel inside here.

2nd stage rocket

Underneath the spacecraft there are two rockets, on top of each other. They are called stages.

1st stage rocket

The stages work one at a time. They fall off when they have used up all their fuel. This makes the load lighter for the next rocket to carry.

How rockets work

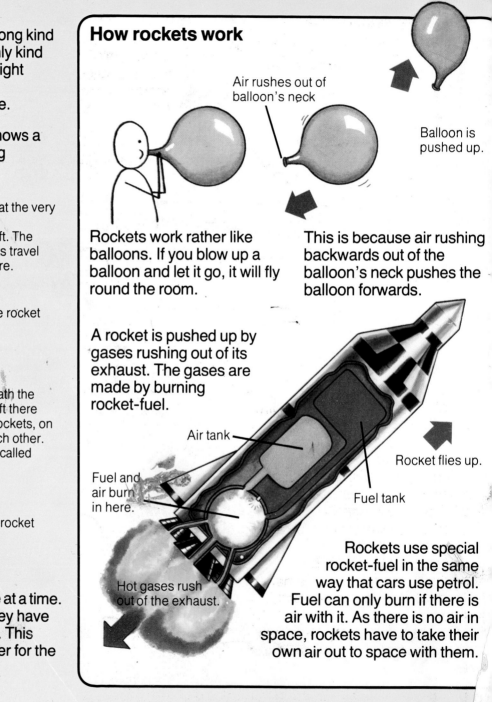

Air rushes out of balloon's neck

Balloon is pushed up.

Rockets work rather like balloons. If you blow up a balloon and let it go, it will fly round the room.

This is because air rushing backwards out of the balloon's neck pushes the balloon forwards.

A rocket is pushed up by gases rushing out of its exhaust. The gases are made by burning rocket-fuel.

Air tank

Fuel and air burn in here.

Rocket flies up.

Fuel tank

Hot gases rush out of the exhaust.

Rockets use special rocket-fuel in the same way that cars use petrol. Fuel can only burn if there is air with it. As there is no air in space, rockets have to take their own air out to space with them.

This picture shows the journey made by the spacecraft Gemini 4 in 1965. The spacecraft was launched into orbit round the Earth. One astronaut made a space walk. Gemini 4 returned to Earth after four days in space.

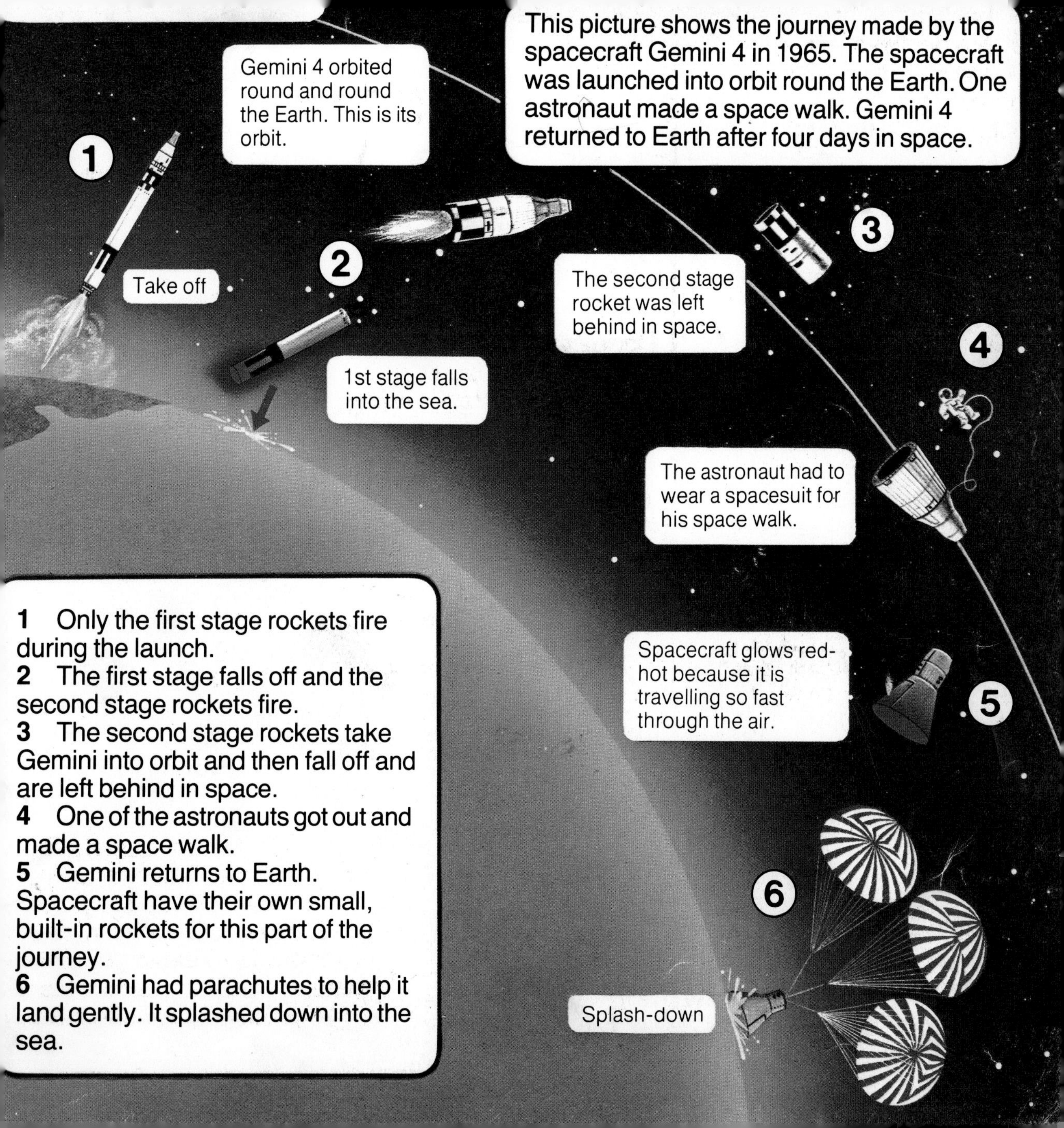

Gemini 4 orbited round and round the Earth. This is its orbit.

1

Take off

2

1st stage falls into the sea.

3

The second stage rocket was left behind in space.

4

The astronaut had to wear a spacesuit for his space walk.

Spacecraft glows red-hot because it is travelling so fast through the air.

5

6

Splash-down

1 Only the first stage rockets fire during the launch.
2 The first stage falls off and the second stage rockets fire.
3 The second stage rockets take Gemini into orbit and then fall off and are left behind in space.
4 One of the astronauts got out and made a space walk.
5 Gemini returns to Earth. Spacecraft have their own small, built-in rockets for this part of the journey.
6 Gemini had parachutes to help it land gently. It splashed down into the sea.

Mission to the Moon

One of the most exciting space missions was the first manned landing on the Moon. It took place in 1969. This gigantic, three stage rocket took the three astronauts in the Apollo spacecraft to the Moon. Since then, five other manned Apollo spacecraft have landed on the Moon.

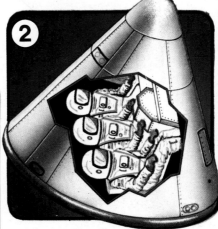

1st stage rocket

2nd stage rocket

The Lunar Module

The astronauts travelled in the Apollo Command Module. This orbited round the Moon, but did not land on it. A special, small spacecraft, called the Lunar Module, landed the astronauts on the Moon. The Lunar Module was stored behind the Apollo Command Module.

The Apollo spacecraft was launched by a huge three stage rocket, called a Saturn 5.

This picture shows the three astronauts inside the tiny Apollo Command Module. It is the only part which returned to Earth.

The trip to the Moon took about three days. On the way the astronauts took the Lunar Module out of storage. The third stage of the Saturn rocket and the Lunar Module storage compartment are left behind in space.

d stage rocket — Apollo spacecraft

Apollo Command Module

This launch escape rocket takes the Command Module to safety if there is an accident at take-off.

The Lunar Module is stored inside here.

4

5

6

Two of the astronauts got into the Lunar Module and flew it to the Moon. Here it is landing. It has its own small, built-in rockets.

After exploring on the Moon the astronauts returned to the Command Module. It had stayed in orbit above the Moon with one astronaut on board.

The bottom part of the Lunar Module was left behind on the Moon. Only the top part took off and flew back to the Apollo Command Module.

The Lunar Module was left behind in space. The three astronauts flew home in the Command Module. It had small rockets of its own too.

On the Moon

The fourth Apollo Moon mission took a moon-buggy, so that the astronauts could explore further.

The astronauts had to wear spacesuits when they were on the Moon. Look on the next page to find out about spacesuits.

Lunar Module

Astronaut

Moon buggy

7

Spacesuits

Astronauts do not have to wear special spacesuits when they are on board their spacecraft. They have to put them on if they go outside into space or on the Moon or another planet. There is no air to breathe in space. It hotter than an oven in the Sun's light, but colder than a freezer in the shade. This pictur shows two astronauts in space.

Astronauts sometimes have to leave their spacecraft to do repairs or set up experiments.

They wear spacesui and are connected their spacecraft b long cable

The spacesuit has a tanks. It also keeps th astronaut at the rig temperature

Putting on a spacesuit

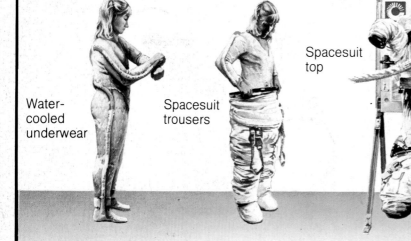

Water-cooled underwear

Spacesuit trousers

Spacesuit top

Helmet goes on last.

Astronauts wear special underwear under their spacesuits. There are tubes going through the material. These carry water round to keep the temperature steady.

Spacesuits are rather bulky and hard to put on. The astronaut puts the trousers on first and then climbs into the top while it is still hanging up.

This is the spacesuit worn by the Shuttle astronauts. Look on the next page to find out about the Shuttle.

Flight cap
Ear-phones
Microphone
Bubble helmet
Outer helmet
Gold layer

This outer helmet goes on top of the bubble helmet. The front is covered with a thin layer of real gold which acts like sunglasses.

The airtanks and radio are inside this big backpack. It is fixed to the suit top. It has enough air for seven hours.

Backpack

Astronauts wearing spacesuits talk to each other by radio. Their caps have a microphone and earphones. A clear bubble helmet goes over the head and joins up to the suit. It fills with air for the astronaut to breathe.

The backpack also pumps the water round the underwear.

Glove

Astronauts can even go to the toilet as the spacesuit has a kind of nappy inside.

The suit has a tiny computer which makes sure that everything is working. It tells the astronaut if anything breaks down and shows how to mend the fault.

Shoes

Spacesuits are made from very tough materials, so they do not tear easily.

Floating in space like this is a very strange feeling. Astronauts have said that it feels a bit like swimming in deep, still water.

This cable keeps the astronaut attached to the spacecraft. It is covered in thin gold.

Cable

9

Space Shuttle

The Shuttle is the newest kind of spacecraft. It is the first one which can be used more than once. It will fly out to space and back to Earth many times.

These are the Shuttle's three main engines. It has other smaller ones.

The Shuttle is the first spacecraft to have wings. They help it to glide back to Earth.

Rocket exhaust

These doors open when the Shuttle is out in space. This helps to keep the spacecraft cool and exposes the special equipment inside.

United States

The storage area is inside here.

Wing

Flying the Shuttle

1

The Shuttle has its own rockets but needs two big booster rockets and an extra fuel tank to launch it into space.

2

The booster rockets and fuel tank fall off when they run out of fuel. The boosters can be used more than once too.

3

The Shuttle has a large storage area for taking things up into space. It can open up when the Shuttle is in orbit.

10

This picture shows parts of the Shuttle cut away, so that you can see inside.

The living-quarters and flight-deck are inside the small nose part of the Shuttle.

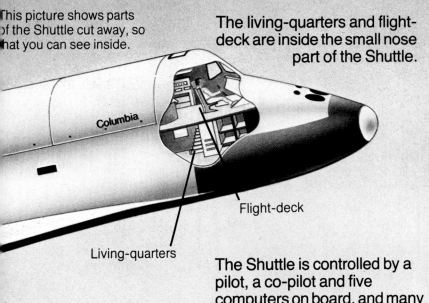

Columbia

Flight-deck

Living-quarters

Special tiles on the outside help to keep the Shuttle cool.

The Shuttle is controlled by a pilot, a co-pilot and five computers on board, and many people at mission-control on Earth.

Shuttle missions

The Shuttle will be used to put new satellites into orbit and bring old or broken ones to Earth.

The Shuttle is planned to take this big telescope into orbit round the Earth. It will be used to study the stars and is controlled from Earth.

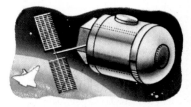

The Shuttle is also booked to take scientists and a laboratory out to orbit and back again. They will do lots of experiments in space.

④ The Shuttle returns to Earth like a glider. It falls though the air glowing red-hot because it is going at high speed.

⑤ It lands like an ordinary plane, on a very long runway. The Shuttle takes only one hour to come to Earth from space.

On board a spacecraft

One of the strangest things about being in space is that everything becomes completely weightless because there is no gravity. There is no "up" or "down". Things will just float in mid-air unless they are fixed to something.

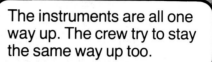
Control instruments

Astronauts sleep in sleeping bags fixed to the "walls". They cannot lie down as they are weightless.

The instruments are all one way up. The crew try to stay the same way up too.

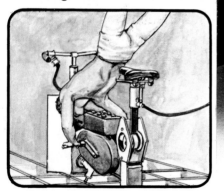

Weightlessness makes the muscles weak. The astronauts use exercise machines to keep fit and healthy.

Astronauts have to hold the special handles when they are doing things, otherwise they push themselves into mid-air.

The spacecraft is controlled most of the time by people at mission control on Earth. The astronauts can take over if necessary.

Space travel makes some astronauts feel sick at first. This may be because they are weightless.

This is a storage area for equipment. Things have to be put away inside cupboards, otherwise they will float around in the spacecraft.

Handles

Astronauts eat ordinary food packed in cans which they heat up in a tray. They have to be careful that the food does not float away.

Food tray

Even liquids float in space. Astronauts have to suck their drinks out of tubes as they cannot use cups.

Baths are a problem. The astronauts shower inside a big bag which stops the water flying about.

The weightless astronauts move by pushing against the walls and using handles. They seem to be flying.

Space station Skylab

A space station is a spacecraft big enough for a crew to live and work in for several weeks. This is the space station Skylab. It was launched into orbit round Earth in 1973.

Space stations stay in orbit a of the time, even when there i no crew on board. Three crews visited Skylab. Each one stayed in space for 56 days.

This is a telescope for studying the Sun.

The Skylab crews did lots of scientific experiments. The most important was to show that people could live in space for a long time.

Skylab was the biggest spacecraft ever made. Inside it was as large as a three-storey house.

These solar panel powered th telescope

Sunshade

This solar panel powered electrical equipment inside Skylab. There should have been another one on the othe side.

Solar panel

Skylab was damaged when it was launched. One of the solar panels and part of the protective outer skin were torn off.

The first crew had to repair Skylab. They put up a sunshade over the damaged outer skin, to stop Skylab overheating.
  The second crew put up this gold foil sunshade.

The astronauts and equipment are inside this part of Skylab.

Going to Skylab

The astronauts got into Skylab through doors here.

Skylab

Apollo spacecraft

Skylab was launched without a crew. The astronauts went up to it and back again in Apollo spacecraft, like the ones which went to the Moon.

The Apollo had to be joined to Skylab. This is called docking. The astronauts crawled into Skylab through special doors in the Apollo and Skylab.

Skylab's end

Skylab was in a low orbit close to Earth. Gravity was able to pull it back to Earth in 1979 after six years in space. The spacecraft broke into

pieces as it fell through the air. Most of the pieces burnt up before reaching Earth. A few fell into the sea and some landed in Australia.

Working on Skylab

The crews did lots of work in Skylab. Here are some of the experiments and studies they did.

One crew studied the comet Kohoutek which passed close to Earth in 1973.

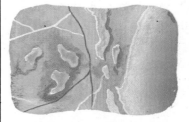

This picture shows a view of Earth from Skylab. The crews took thousands of photographs of the Earth and Sun.

One crew took a spider into space to see if it could spin a web while weightless. The first one was not very good, but later ones were better.

Satellites

There are many small, unmanned spacecraft in orbit close to the Earth. They are called satellites. Satellites carry instruments and do lots of useful jobs. This picture shows a satellite called Landsat. It studies the Earth.

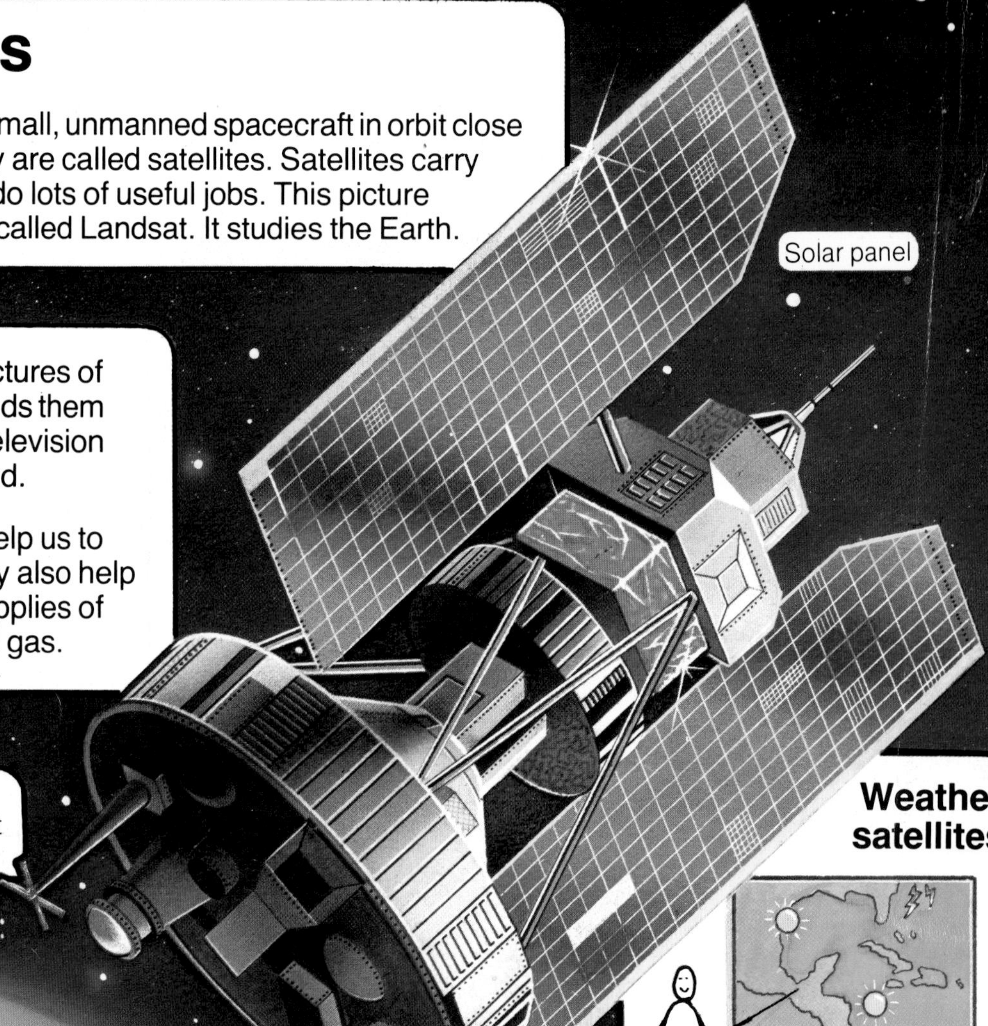

Solar panel

Landsat takes pictures of the Earth and sends them down to special television sets on the ground.

These pictures help us to make maps. They also help us to find new supplies of things like oil and gas.

Landsat's cameras and instruments point down towards Earth.

Weather satellites

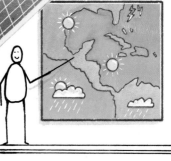

Other satellites watch the weather. They help scientists to make the weather forecasts.

Satellites have solar panels to provide power for their instruments. The solar panels make electricity from sunlight.

elevision by satellite

1 Several satellites are used to send television pictures from one part of the world to another. The pictures are sent as radio signals.

2 These signals are beamed up through space to the satellite. They bounce off the satellite and back to Earth, but to a different place.

3 The signals are picked up on Earth by big dish-shaped aerials like the one above. The satellite has dish-shaped aerials as well.

4 The signals are then sent to your television set and turned back into pictures. The whole journey takes just a few seconds.

Going round the Earth

The Earth spins round once every day.

Television satellites move in time with the Earth. This means that they stay above the same place all the time.

Satellites which study the Earth orbit much faster. They see the whole world once every few hours.

Visiting the planets

People have travelled in space only as far as our Moon. Unmanned spacecraft, called probes, are used to explore the planets, as these are very far away.

This is Voyager 2, a probe that went to Jupiter in 1979 and Saturn in 1981.

Probes are launched into space by rockets.

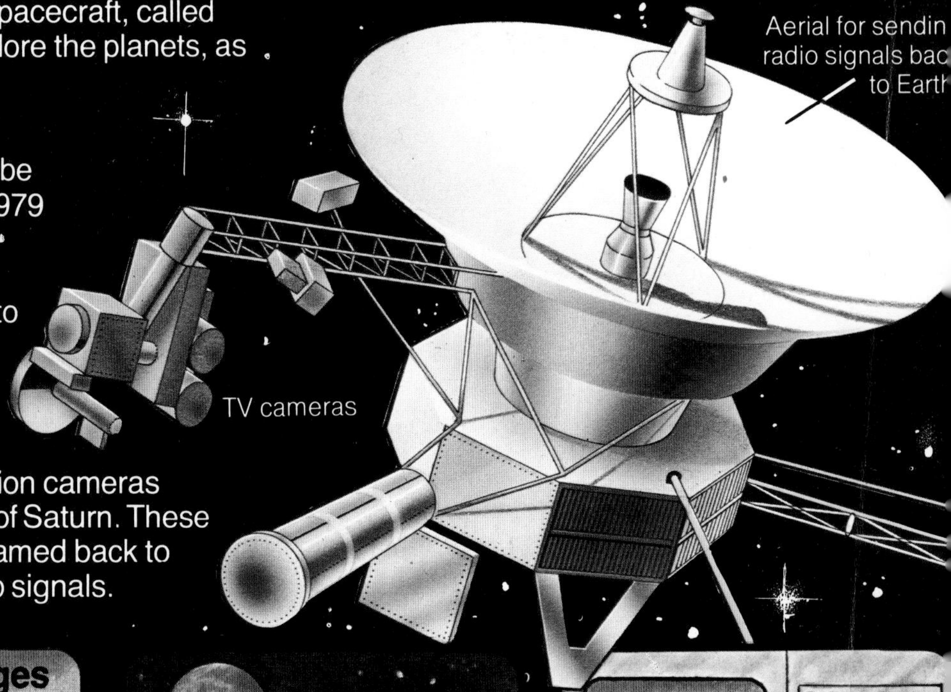

Aerial for sending radio signals back to Earth

TV cameras

These television cameras took pictures of Saturn. These were then beamed back to Earth as radio signals.

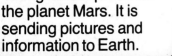

Messages from Mars

Mars

Earth

This picture shows the Viking lander probe on the planet Mars. It is sending pictures and information to Earth.

The information and pictures travel across space as radio signals. They take 20 minutes to reach Earth from Mars.

Here are scientists studying the pictures and information from the probe on Mars. They are using a computer.

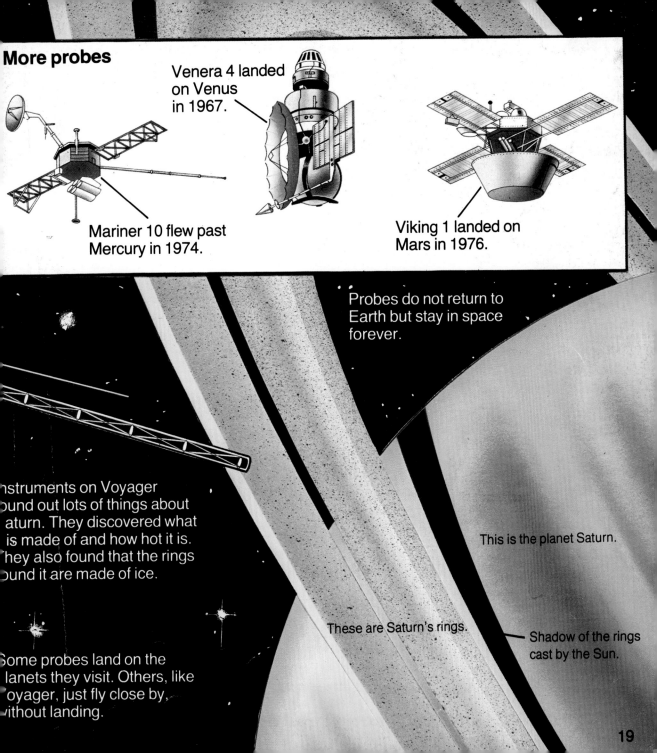

More probes

Venera 4 landed on Venus in 1967.

Mariner 10 flew past Mercury in 1974.

Viking 1 landed on Mars in 1976.

Probes do not return to Earth but stay in space forever.

nstruments on Voyager
ound out lots of things about
aturn. They discovered what
is made of and how hot it is.
hey also found that the rings
ound it are made of ice.

This is the planet Saturn.

These are Saturn's rings.

Shadow of the rings cast by the Sun.

ome probes land on the
lanets they visit. Others, like
oyager, just fly close by,
ithout landing.

The future in space

One day people may live and work in huge space cities like the one pictured here. It is about as big as New York and not at all like a spacecraft. The space city has artificial gravity and is full of air in the parts where people live. There are houses, parks, farms, offices, schools, factories, shops and even sports centres – in fact, everything that people want.

The space city would have solar panels to make electricity from sunlight.

Satellites would be used for sending messages between the Earth and the space city.

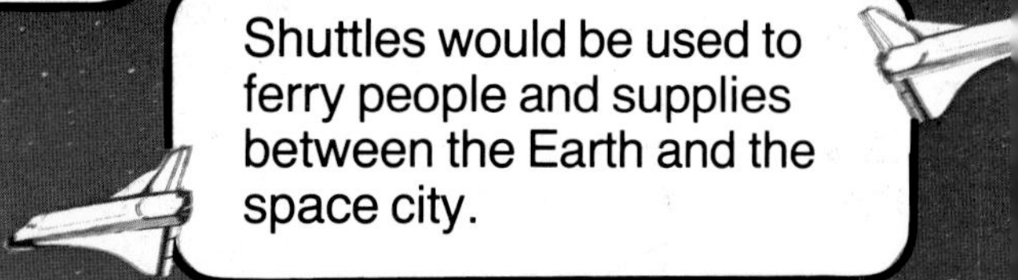

Shuttles would be used to ferry people and supplies between the Earth and the space city.

In the future, we may put large solar panels into space. These would make electricity from sunlight and beam it down to Earth.

Inside a space city

The sky would look slightly different from a space city. You would be able to see Earth and would have a different view of the Moon.

This picture shows what it could be like inside a space city. This is the ring-shaped part where people live. It has gravity, air, plants, buildings and even a river. There are big windows to let in sunlight and heat.

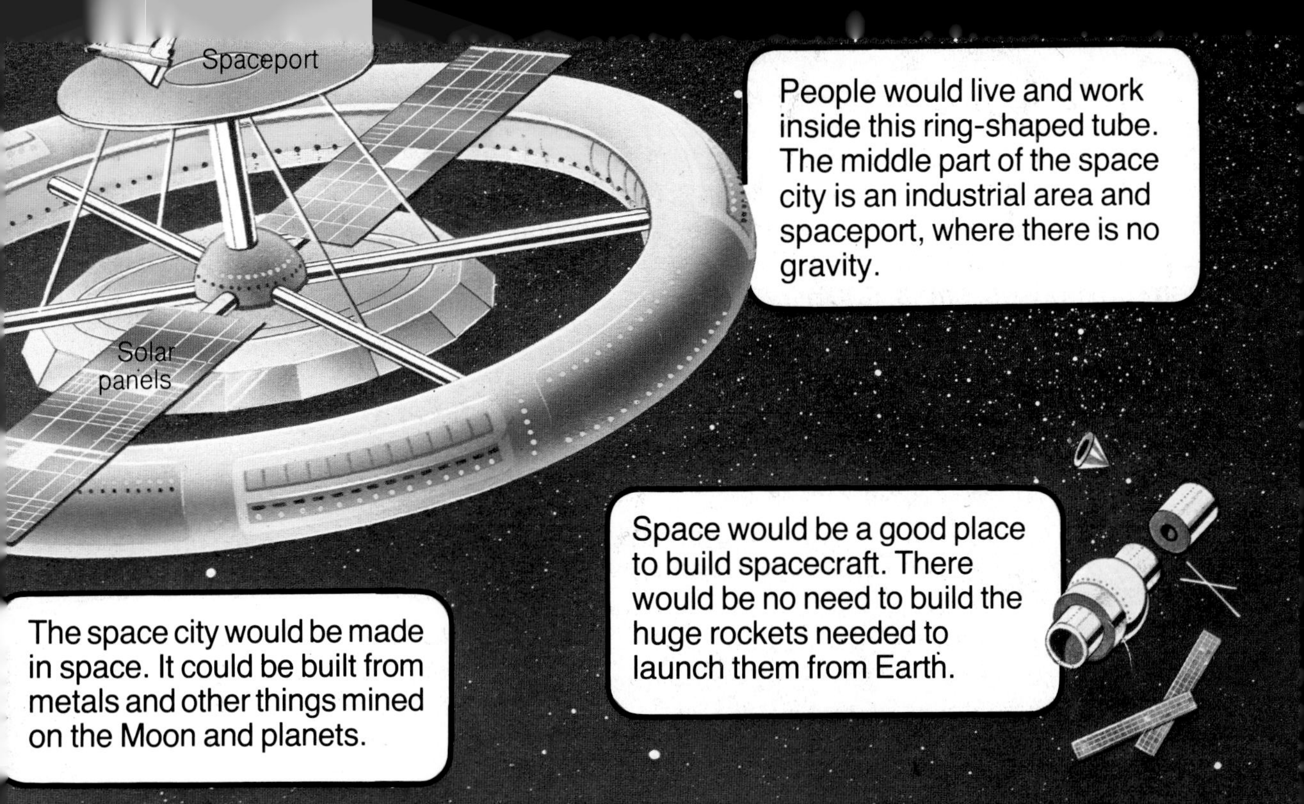

Spaceport

Solar panels

People would live and work inside this ring-shaped tube. The middle part of the space city is an industrial area and spaceport, where there is no gravity.

Space would be a good place to build spacecraft. There would be no need to build the huge rockets needed to launch them from Earth.

The space city would be made in space. It could be built from metals and other things mined on the Moon and planets.

Living on Mars

People would have to wear spacesuits if they went outside the city.

This picture shows what a city on Mars might be like. It is built under domes that are filled with air and kept warm. There is little air on Mars and it gets very cold. A colony on the Moon could be similar to this one.

Star travel fantasy

This picture shows what a spacecraft of the future might be like. It has left our Solar System and is travelling to another star. Scientists think that there could be a planet rather like Earth there.

At the moment star travel seems to be impossible. This is because the stars are so very far away. It would take much longer than person's lifetime to travel to them in the spacecraft which we have today.

Even the nearest star is too far away to visit. If stone age people had been able to make a spacecraft and set out on a journey to the nearest star, they would be only about half way there by now, 50,000 years later.

Perhaps the crew of a star ship could be frozen or put into a deep sleep for the long journey to the stars. Computers and robots might look after the spacecraft and wake up the crew when they arrived.

Going through a space warp

People who write stories about space and some scientists have thought about the problems of star travel. They have imagined new ways of travelling through space. This picture shows one idea – a space warp.

The space warp is like a hole in space. The star ship goes into the hole in one part of space, but comes out again in a completely different place. The whole journey could take just a few seconds.

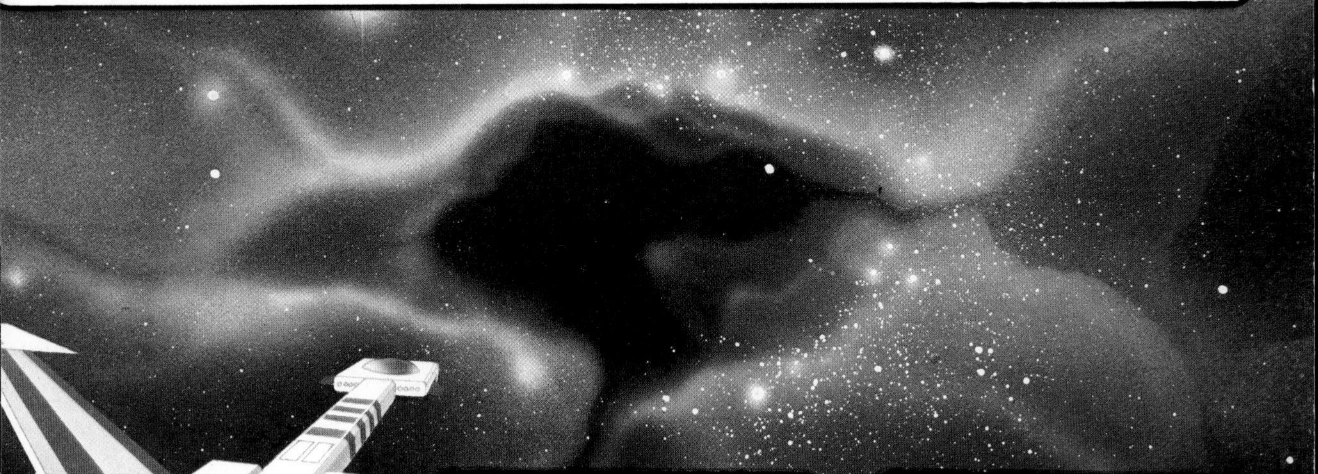

Travelling space city

Perhaps people will go to other stars in huge travelling space cities. Many people would be born, have children and die before arriving.

Beaming through space

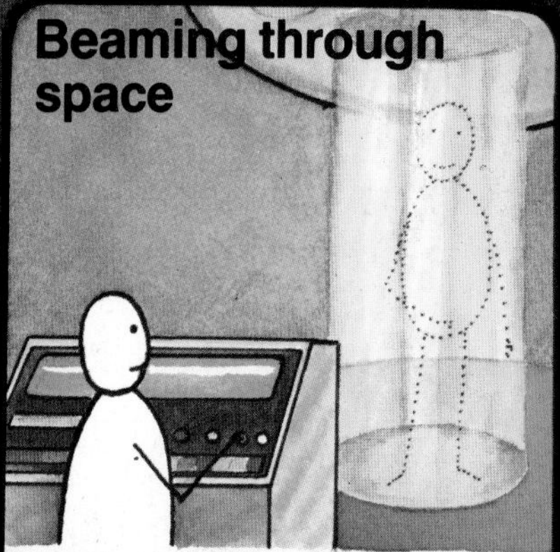

Another idea is to beam people through space. They would be broken down into tiny specks for the journey and joined together at the other end.

Index